Folens

Book 1

LANGUAGE WORKS

Contents

The Musicians of Bremen

There once was a donkey living near the town of Bremen who was getting too old to work. He knew his master would soon stop feeding him so he <u>decided</u> to join the <u>musicians</u> who lived in Bremen. On his way, he met a dog who was getting too old to hunt and whose master was going to kill him. The donkey asked the dog to go with him to Bremen. The two new friends then met a cat who had overheard her master saying that he was going to drown her, and a cock whose mistress was about to use him for soup. "Join us," said the donkey and off they all <u>trooped</u> to Bremen.

That night the animals rested in a forest. From a high branch, the cock spotted a cottage in the <u>distance</u> and led his friends there in search of food. Through the window, they saw a band of robbers sitting at a table which was covered with things to eat. The animals climbed on top of each other, started singing and <u>tumbled</u> in through the window. The robbers were so frightened they ran away. The animals ate their fill, turned out the light and went to sleep.

The robbers hid in the forest. When the light went out, the bravest one returned to the house and crept inside. He saw two sparks glowing in the fireplace and blew on them to make some light. Out jumped the cat, spitting and scratching. The robber <u>stumbled</u> backwards onto the dog's paw. The dog bit his leg. The robber ran out screaming. In the yard, the donkey kicked him and the cock crowed in a <u>piercing</u> tone.

The robber ran back to his gang. He was terrified. "A witch lives in that house; she scratched me. Then a monster bit me on the legs and another creature screamed at me," he cried. On hearing this, the robbers fled. The animals continued to live happily in their new home.

A ▸ **Answer these questions.**

1. Why did the donkey think his master wouldn't feed him?
2. Who saw the cottage first?
3. How do you think the animals knew the people were robbers?
4. What did the animals do to get the robbers out of the house?
5. Why do you think the robber returned?
6. The sparks in the fireplace were not cinders. What were they?
7. Who did the robber think lived in the house?
8. How does the story show the animals were friends?
9. Use your dictionary to explain the underlined words.

B ▸ **All stories contain something useful. What do you think we can learn from this story?**

Write a paragraph explaining what you think.

C ▸ **Read the story carefully again and, using your own words:**

1. Write a description of the animals travelling to Bremen. What would the road be like? What time of day would it be?
2. Now write what the forest and the robbers' cottage would be like. Remember it will be night-time.

D ▸ **Write the beginning of the story, where all the animals meet each other, as a playscript.**

Start like this and set your work out correctly.
Scene 1
A donkey knows his master will not feed him once he is too old to work. He decides to run away. On the way he meets some other animals.

Donkey: I see you are getting too old to hunt. How will your master treat you?
Dog: ...

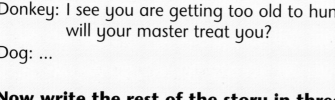

E ▸ **Now write the rest of the story in three more scenes.**

Read your play with a partner.

5

Syllables (1)

● A word can be divided into two syllables, if there are two of the same consonants in the middle of it and if there are vowels before and after the consonants.

 Read aloud.

sum/mer, rob/ber, ten/nis, rub/ber, nug/get, sud/den, slip/per

 Match the first syllable with the second syllable and write the new word. Write a sentence for each word.

A	B		A	B
win	rot		hor	bit
mut	ner		rab	low
yel	ror		cot	ten
car	per		nar	ror
mir	ton		kit	ton
pep	low		hol	row

There are 18 words in the wordsearch. How many can you find?

x	h	p	p	l	b	h	s	y	a	l	k	s
e	o	z	o	c	l	i	t	t	e	r	y	t
o	p	s	n	r	e	d	y	e	d	o	t	o
h	p	u	r	j	u	d	d	e	r	t	d	p
l	e	t	t	e	r	e	o	w	o	t	s	p
p	r	i	b	b	o	n	l	r	b	e	h	e
u	x	q	i	g	i	w	u	j	b	n	o	r
s	j	i	g	l	i	n	h	d	e	e	p	b
m	a	f	g	p	n	h	i	f	r	f	p	a
a	l	r	e	e	q	i	u	l	c	j	i	t
l	d	k	r	w	d	c	s	n	x	l	n	t
l	e	r	q	o	t	c	a	b	b	a	g	e
e	r	e	u	v	w	u	v	m	j	q	j	r
r	n	w	g	z	i	p	p	e	r	w	h	i

hopper	litter
zipper	rotten
hiccup	stopper
arrow	letter
shopping	batter
runner	udder
cabbage	ribbon
robber	bigger
hidden	smaller

Vowel Sounds

A **Look at the ai words below. The a does the talking. Read them aloud.**

● When two vowels go out walking the first one does the talking.

rail, pail, mail, tail, frail, bait, faith, braille, trait.
Write each word in a sentence.

B **Look at the words below. The e does the talking. Read them aloud.**

read, lead, meal, feet, sheet, weed.

C **Choose the correct word to complete these sentences.**

1. My shoe was tight and it hurt my (*heel/heal*).
2. Next (*weak/week*) we are going on holiday.
3. My sister does not eat (*meat/meet*).
4. Did the boy (*steel/steal*) the pen?
5. I will (*see/sea*) you in the morning.

D **oa and ow have the same sound in some words. Read these words aloud (o does the talking).**

boat, moat, roar, low, mow, crow.

E **Look at the pictures below. Say each word aloud. Write the words in two lists, those with ow and with oa.**

 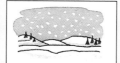   

   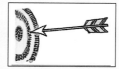 

Capital Letters (1)

I am very important.

I always have a capital letter.

● When **I** is on its own, it always has a capital letter.

A **Rewrite these sentences, using a capital I where appropriate.**

1. i do not like children in my garden.
2. The sun said, "i am angry with the giant."
3. i was sad when i couldn't play in the garden.
4. If i were taller i could climb the tree.
5. Now i will take you to my garden.

B **The flower is angry because its capital letters are missing. Can you replace them?**

1. i started life as a tiny seed.
2. alan planted me in the garden last april.
3. he dug a hole and placed me in it.
4. his mother, anne, reminded him to water me.
5. every wednesday alan checked to see if i was growing.
6. then one day little green shoots appeared.
7. alan's friends, vicky and paul, came to see me.
8. soon i had leaves and little buds.
9. i was getting big and strong.
10. in june i became a fully grown flower.

About Me

 A Draw your own family tree.

How far can you go back?

 B Write more about yourself.

Describe yourself, your height, weight, eye colour, hair colour, etc. Describe your favourite food, drink, clothes, games. What bores you? What interests you? What are your hobbies?

 C Write a paragraph about your best friend.

Describe him/her. What is his/her name?
What do you do together?
What annoys you about your friend?
Explain why this person is your best friend.

 D Write about the time when you were the new child.

Being the new child can be tough!
Write about a time when you were new. Maybe you joined a club. Maybe you moved house, started at a new school and had to make friends. How did it feel? What is not nice about being new? How can you make friends? How can the people in charge of the group help? What can other children do to make you feel you belong?

The Selfish Giant

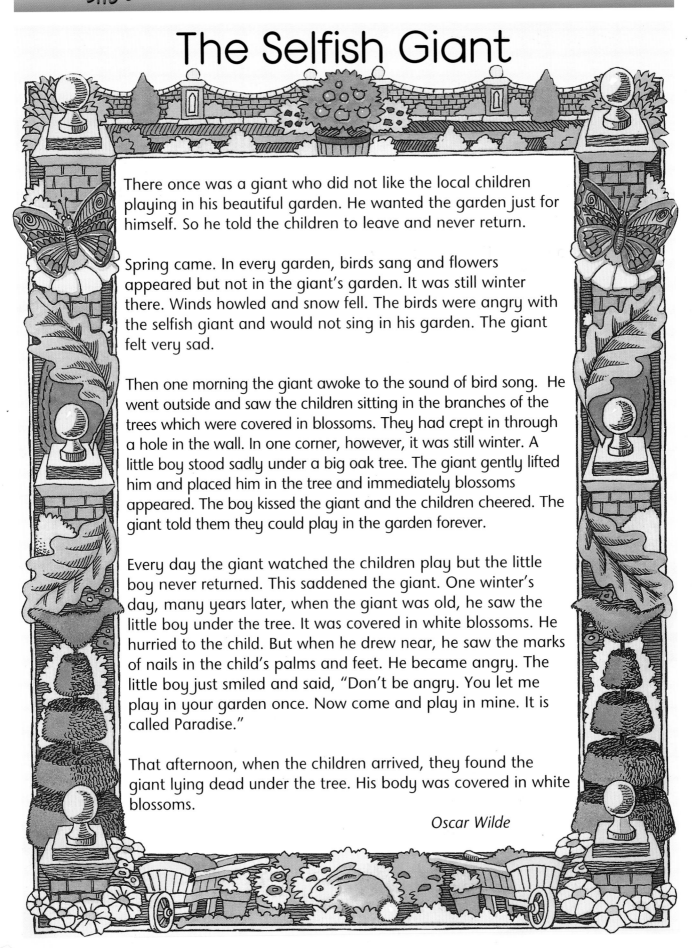

There once was a giant who did not like the local children playing in his beautiful garden. He wanted the garden just for himself. So he told the children to leave and never return.

Spring came. In every garden, birds sang and flowers appeared but not in the giant's garden. It was still winter there. Winds howled and snow fell. The birds were angry with the selfish giant and would not sing in his garden. The giant felt very sad.

Then one morning the giant awoke to the sound of bird song. He went outside and saw the children sitting in the branches of the trees which were covered in blossoms. They had crept in through a hole in the wall. In one corner, however, it was still winter. A little boy stood sadly under a big oak tree. The giant gently lifted him and placed him in the tree and immediately blossoms appeared. The boy kissed the giant and the children cheered. The giant told them they could play in the garden forever.

Every day the giant watched the children play but the little boy never returned. This saddened the giant. One winter's day, many years later, when the giant was old, he saw the little boy under the tree. It was covered in white blossoms. He hurried to the child. But when he drew near, he saw the marks of nails in the child's palms and feet. He became angry. The little boy just smiled and said, "Don't be angry. You let me play in your garden once. Now come and play in mine. It is called Paradise."

That afternoon, when the children arrived, they found the giant lying dead under the tree. His body was covered in white blossoms.

Oscar Wilde

Answer these questions.

1. Why did the giant tell the children to leave his garden?

2. Why did the birds stop singing in the garden?

3. Why do you think the little boy was not able to climb the tree.

4. When the children arrived in the afternoon, what did they find?

5. When the children returned, the blossoms appeared. Why do you think this happened?

6. Where is the garden of Paradise?

7. Who do you think the child was?

 Focus on the giant.

1. The giant had different sides to him. Find words and phrases in the story that tell you what he was like.

2. The giant also learned new things. What do you think these were?

3. Write a paragraph about the giant using the information from 1. and 2.

 Write down your own words to describe these lines of the story.

'Winds howled and snow fell.'

'... the trees were covered in blossoms.'

'... the children cheered.'

'It is called Paradise.'

Choose one line and use your words to write your own description.
Begin 'There was once..'

D **See if you can find the full story of 'The Selfish Giant' by Oscar Wilde in the library and read it.**

How does Oscar Wilde use the description of colour to affect our feelings?

Sounds – Soft c and Hard c

- Before **e**, **i** or **y**, **c** sounds like **s** (a soft sound).
- Before any other letter, **c** sounds like **k** (a hard sound).

A **Write out the words below, putting c in each. Read each word aloud. Some have a soft sound. Some have a hard sound.**

 mi _ e

 _ ream

 _ amel

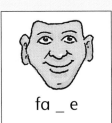 fa _ e

 pen _ il

 _ rane

 _ ar

 prin _ e

 _ amera

 _ anoe

B **Now write the words in two lists: those with a soft c and those with a hard c.**

Soft c	Hard c
mice	cream

C **Use words from the box to finish each sentence. Read them aloud.**

1. The _____ is in the cage.
2. I threw the _____ and got a six.
3. We put _____ in the salad.
4. Mum lit the _____ .
5. London is a big _____ .
6. Mary put on her _____ .

| candle |
| canary |
| dice |
| city |
| lettuce |
| necklace |

Sounds – Soft g and Hard g

- Before **e**, **i** or **y**, **g** sounds like **j** (a soft sound).
- Before any other letter, **g** has a hard sound.

A **Write out the words below, putting the g in each. Read each one aloud. Some have a soft sound. Some have a hard sound.**

_ iraffe

_ lass

brid _ e

_ un

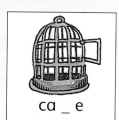

ca _ e

le _

_ ypsy

ba _

_ iant

_ uitar

B **Now write the words in two lists:
those with a soft g and those with a hard g.**

Soft g	Hard g
giraffe	glass

C **Use words from the box to finish each sentence. Read them aloud.**

1. Dad threw a _____ on the fire.
2. _____ sweets are nice.
3. The actor was on the _____ .
4. We had _____ fun on our tour.
5. I would like to _____ home now.
6. The _____ is a very tall animal.

stage
great
fudge
go
giraffe
log

13

Capital Letters (2)

- Can you remember when to use a capital letter?

1. At the start of a sentence.
2. For names of people, personal titles and places.
3. For the name of a day and a month.
4. For the pronoun 'I'.
5. For headings and book titles.

 Rewrite these sentences, putting in capital letters.

1. at first the giant was selfish.
2. my birthday is in april.
3. my teacher is called mrs phipps.
4. on holiday in spain i read 'charlie and the chocolate factory' by roald dahl.
5. on sunday i go swimming with baljit.
6. i ran away when my mum told me to shut up!
7. tomorrow i am going to london to visit the natural history museum.
8. on wednesday i got measles and dr richards said i could have a whole week off school!

 Solve the clue. The answer is in the train. Remember your capital letters!

1. londonamsterdambremenbristol
   The capital city of England is _____ .

2. mondaythursdaysaturday
   The weekend starts on _____ .

3. maydecembermarchapril
   Christmas is in _____ .

4. dublinlondoncardiffedinburgh
   The capital city of Scotland is _____ .

Overused Words

● Some words are used too often. Let us see what alternatives we can find to help us write more interesting sentences.

 A **Write out the sentences below with one of the new words instead of went.**

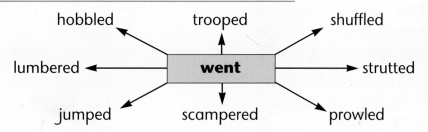

hobbled   trooped   shuffled

lumbered ← **went** → strutted

jumped   scampered   prowled

1. The elephants _____ through the forest.
2. The mouse _____ across the floor.
3. The tiger _____ through the undergrowth.
4. The proud peacock _____ as the frog _____ across its path.
5. The polar bear _____ through the snow.
6. The injured hunter _____ to the jeep.
7. The old man _____ down the path.

 B **Write out the sentences below with one of the new words instead of nice.**

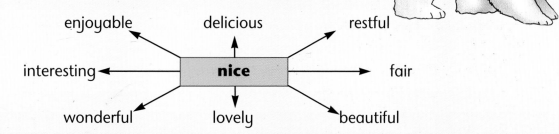

enjoyable   delicious   restful

interesting ← **nice** → fair

wonderful   lovely   beautiful

1. We had a _____ meal.
2. I spent a _____ afternoon reading an _____ book.
3. The weather was _____ and we had an _____ day.
4. She is a very _____ baby.
5. We went for a _____ long walk in the mountains.
6. "How _____ , you've brought me flowers!" she exclaimed.

The Emperor's New Clothes

Once there lived a vain emperor. He cared about nothing except his clothes. One day two rogues came to town and set up as weavers. They told everyone that their clothes were beautiful, with exquisite colours. They also said that only intelligent people could see the material. The emperor soon heard about this and decided he must have a suit made from this material. He ordered the rogues to make him a suit of clothes for a special procession and paid them lots of gold. He also gave them gold threads and fine silks. All of these went into their pockets. The weavers set up their looms and started to work.

Soon the emperor was curious, so he sent an old, loyal minister to have a look. To the minister's horror, he could see nothing on the loom. As he was afraid he would lose his job he pretended he could see the beautiful cloth pointed to by the weavers. The emperor soon sent another official. The same thing happened.

On the eve of the procession, the weavers worked through the night pretending to sew and cut. The morning of the procession dawned. The emperor and his courtiers arrived. To his dismay the emperor could see nothing, but he couldn't let anyone know that. He undressed, put on his new clothes and everyone said how splendid he looked. Soon the procession began.

The emperor walked under a large canopy. All the people called out, "How beautiful the emperor's new clothes are." No one wanted to say they could see no clothes.

Then a child shouted, "But he has nothing on!"

One person whispered to another and soon everyone cried, "Look at the emperor! He has nothing on!"

Hans Christian Andersen

A **Answer these questions.**

1. Who did the rogues say could see the clothes they made?
2. Why did the emperor decide to get a suit made?
3. Explain why the minister lied to the emperor.
4. Why do you think the emperor didn't inspect the work?
5. Do you think the emperor was 'intelligent'? Explain your answer.
6. What did the rogues do the night before the procession?
7. What do you think happens next in the story?
8. There is a message for us in this story. What do you think it is? Write down your answer.
9. Find these words in the story and write down what you think they mean. Check your answers in a dictionary:
   Paragraph 1: vain, emperor, rogue, weavers, exquisite, procession, looms.
   Paragraph 2: curious, minister.
   Paragraph 3: courtiers, dismay.
   Paragraph 4: canopy.

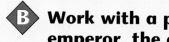 **B** **Work with a partner. One should be the emperor, the other should be a minister.**

Work out a dialogue to say aloud, in which the emperor is telling the minister to find out how the weavers are getting on.

Choose voices to suit the characters.

Now do the same and work out a dialogue between the minister and one of the weavers. How does the minister's voice change?

C **Read the last part of the story again.**
Look at the dialogue and complete these questions.

1. What punctuation do we use to show someone is speaking?
2. Write down a statement that is spoken.
3. Write down a sentence that is spoken which has an exclamation mark.
4. What happens to the sentences when someone new speaks?

 D **Retell the story using a modern setting.**
Think about how it would be different today.

Prefixes (1)

- A prefix is a letter or a group of letters placed before a root word, so as to change its meaning. Look at what these prefixes do.

Prefix	Meaning	Example
1. in-	not, opposite of	incorrect, incapable
2. un-	not, opposite of	unhappy, untie
3. dis-	not, opposite of	disagree, discontent
4. im-	not, opposite of	imperfect, immortal
5. ir-	not, opposite of	irregular, irresistible

 Rewrite the sentences. Combine the correct prefix with the root words below, so as to make sense of each one.

1. The A.A. warned that it was _____ advisable to go near the accident scene.
2. Too many drivers _____ obey the speed restrictions on our roads.
3. The landlady was rude and _____ polite when I introduced myself to her.
4. The torrential showers caused the pitch to be _____ usable.
5. I thought her explanation was _____ rational and I could not understand it.
6. The girl was kind and _____ selfish and gave her seat to the old man.
7. The teacher said my answer was _____ complete, as I hadn't explained everything.

Synonyms and Antonyms

- Antonyms are words that are opposite in meaning.

Match the words that are similar in meaning in columns 1 and 2 (synonyms). Then match with the correct antonyms in column 3.

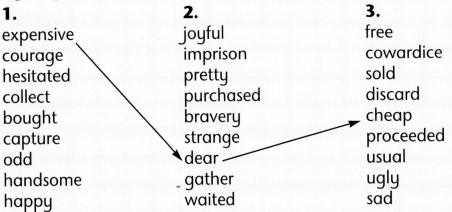

1.	**2.**	**3.**
expensive	joyful	free
courage	imprison	cowardice
hesitated	pretty	sold
collect	purchased	discard
bought	bravery	cheap
capture	strange	proceeded
odd	dear	usual
handsome	gather	ugly
happy	waited	sad

And or But?

- **And** and **but** are conjunctions.
- They can be used to join two sentences, making one more interesting sentence.

The fire raged for two days. It frightened the animals.
The fire raged for two days and frightened the animals.

 A **Join these sentences with and or but. Write your new sentences.**

1. The lion roared. He pounced on his prey.
2. I like jam. I hate marmalade.
3. Rory knocked loudly. Still no one answered.
4. She screamed. No one came.
5. Tina washed up. I dried.
6. I trained hard. I didn't win the race.
7. The cheetah ran. He couldn't escape.
8. Elephants are herbivores. They eat leaves and grass.
9. The chimp threw down the nuts. The ape gathered them.
10. The hunter pointed his gun. He shot the elephant.
11. Mary put on her glasses. She still couldn't see.
12. I wanted new trainers. I didn't have the money.
13. I stood at the quay. I watched the boat set sail.
14. The boys heard the bell. They ran to school.
15. I put on my new dress. It was too small.
16. Jill was tossing and turning. She couldn't sleep.

 B **Read this paragraph.**

It was a crisp winter's morning and I jumped out of bed and dressed quickly. Today we were going to visit our cousins in Manchester and I hurried downstairs and found everyone was waiting for me. Without further delay, I ran to the car and got in and Dad started the engine and we were on our way.

Rewrite this paragraph with fewer 'ands' and more full stops.

Full Stops

- Always end a sentence with a full stop.

A **Not only have the rogues taken the emperor's gold, but they have also taken our full stops! Copy the paragraph and see if you can replace them.**

The rogues were very clever They knew the Emperor could be fooled easily Having taken his gold, they pretended to work hard making his suit They laughed as they sewed While everyone was watching the procession the rogues disappeared

B **Write each paragraph below, inserting capital letters and full stops. The first sentence in each is done for you.**

1. The minister hurried to where the rogues were working. he looked at the loom to his horror he could see nothing the rogues pointed to the beautiful colours and patterns in the cloth the minister pretended he could see them and said the cloth was beautiful

2. The rogues pretended to hand the Emperor his new clothes. first he put on his trousers, then he put on the jacket the rogues attached the train to the new suit the emperor looked in the mirror and pretended to admire himself when he was ready, he went outside and waited until his attendants arrived

• In the story *The Emperor's New Clothes* how did the emperor feel when he realised he had no clothes on? Did he feel angry?

This poem was written by an eight-year-old boy, Ian White.

In it he describes how he feels when he is angry.

When I Am Angry

When I get angry I start
      screaming
and screeching
      raging
and hating
      smashing
and biting
      crying
and punching
      leaving
and breaking
      throwing
and destroying
      steamed up
and blowing up
      slam doors
and stamping
      exploding
and strangling
      cuddling
and kissing
      sorrys
and quiet again.

Ian White (8)

1. What makes you angry? What frightens you?
2. Write a poem called 'When I am frightened'.
   Start it like this: When I am frightened I start shivering...

Danny Fox Steals Some Fish

Danny Fox is very clever. He wanted a free meal and in this passage we find out how he tricked the fisherman and got his dinner!

When the driver saw Danny lying stretched in the middle of the road, he stopped his cart and said, "That's funny. That's the fox that was stealing my fish. That's the fox I hit with my whip. I thought I had only touched the tip of his tail but now I see I must have hurt him badly. He must have run away from me, ahead of my cart. And now he is dead." He got down from his cart and stooped to look at Danny.

"What a beautiful red coat he's got," the driver said, "and what beautiful, thick red trousers. What a beautiful long bushy tail, with a beautiful white tip. What a beautiful long smooth nose with a beautiful black tip. I'll take him home with me, I think, and skin him and sell his fur."

So he picked up Danny Fox and threw him onto the cart on top of the boxes of fish. The cart went on. Danny opened one eye and saw the driver's back was turned to him. Then, very quickly, he slid the tip of his tail underneath a fish and flicked it onto the road. He lay quite still and threw another fish out with his tail, then another and another, till all down the road, behind the cart, there was a long, long line of fish stretching into the distance. And the driver never looked round, because he thought Danny was dead. At the next corner Danny jumped off and ran back down the road. When the cart was out of sight, he started to pick up the fish.

David Thomson

22

 Answer these questions.

1. What did the fisherman do when he saw Danny on the road?
2. Why did he think he was dead?
3. What did the fisherman plan to do with the 'dead' fox?
4. In your own words tell how Danny stole the fish.
5. Why did Danny jump off at a corner?
6. How do you think the fisherman felt when he realised his fish were gone?

 Write a description of Danny. Say what he was like and what he looked like.

 Do you think the story of Danny Fox is fiction or non-fiction?

Write down your answer and say why.
Write down two examples of fiction and two examples of non-fiction.

 Write your own story about Danny Fox. Write three paragraphs to show the beginning, middle and end, like this:

There was once a fox called Danny. He was ...
So, Danny thought to himself, ...
Finally ...

 Now retell the story as if you are Danny Fox.

Begin: I was feeling really hungry when ...

My Diary

● Steve is preparing for an important football match at Wembley. This is the diary of the week before the big event on Saturday.

Monday	*I woke up early today. The sun was shining and I put on my tracksuit for a five-kilometre run. After having a shower I had orange juice and toast for my breakfast. We are playing at Wembley on Saturday so I must train hard to improve my fitness.*
Tuesday	*Today I practised controlling the ball in and out of obstacles. We had to weave our way around an obstacle course and then aim at the goal without stopping. I scored three goals. I felt excited and nervous all at once.*
Wednesday	*The squad ran a fifteen-kilometre jog today and then got into teams to play against each other. I tried to run faster than anyone else and to be in the right place to score a goal.*

 Write Steve's diary entries for Thursday, Friday and Saturday, the day of the match.

Thursday. Today I ...

 Keep a diary for one week.

Record in it what you did each day, who you played with, what you played, how you felt, etc.

Mixed-up Sentences

 Rewrite the sentences in the correct order.

Danny Fox is up to his tricks again!
He has mixed up the sentences in the following stories.

1. He went to the vineyard and saw the juicy grapes.
   The fox was very hungry.
   Try as he could, he wasn't able to reach them.

2. He chased the fox off his land.
   The sly fox crept into the farm.
   The chickens made such a noise, they woke the farmer.

 Rewrite the passages in the correct order.

1. Danny slid the tip of his tail under a fish. When he was finished, Danny jumped off and collected the fish. Danny pretended to be dead. Then he flicked it onto the road. The fisherman threw him onto the cart.

2. They went home happily. They were going to pick blackberries. They could bake a pie now. The briars were laden with fruit and the children soon filled their buckets. The children walked down the country lane.

25

Writing Descriptions

 A **In the passage 'Danny Fox Steals Some Fish', the fisherman gives a lovely description of Danny Fox. Read it aloud.**

"What a beautiful red coat ..."

 B **Now write out the passage, filling in the blanks to describe either a deer or a badger. The words provided should help.**

1. Deer: (reddish-brown coat, long antlers, body, light cream rump, delicate face)
2. Badger: (coat, powerful legs, grey body, black stripe, gentle nose)

What a beautiful _____ he's got. What beautiful _____ . What a beautiful _____ with a beautiful _____ and what a beautiful _____ he has.

C **Write a description of someone in your class.**

Include in your description colour of hair, length of hair, colour of eyes, height, weight, etc. Do not write down the person's name. If your description is good enough the other children in the class should recognise who you have described.

D **Write a letter to a classmate describing yourself. Do not write your name. Sign it, 'Guess Who?'.**

(Check your letter for spelling mistakes, mistakes with capital letters and full stops, before 'posting' it.)
Your teacher will deliver all the letters.
Identify the writers of the mystery letters!

 E **Write a descriptive paragraph for this illustration.**

Questions and Answers

● A question sentence starts with a capital letter and ends with a question mark (?).
Which bird has a red breast? How do birds fly?

 Write out the questions, putting in capital letters and question marks.

    1. where does a squirrel live
    2. what is a baby fox called
    3. what shape is a robin's nest
    4. where does a badger live
    5. which tree gives us acorns
    6. what does the word hibernate mean
    7. what do fish use to breathe
    8. what is a male deer called

Write the answers to the questions.

 The words below are all question words. Choose the correct question word and write out each complete sentence. The answers will help.

What?	Who?	Whose?	Which?
Where?	How?	Why?	When?

Questions

    1. _____ were the animals going?
    2. _____ wrote *The Emperor's New Clothes*?
    3. _____ did the fisherman stop?
    4. _____ was the fox's name?
    5. _____ many eggs does a robin lay?
    6. _____ do we eat mince pies?

Answers

Bremen.
Hans Christian Andersen.
He thought Danny was dead.
Danny.
She lays between three and seven.
At Christmas.

The Olympic Games

The First Olympic Games

The Olympic Games began in Greece almost 28 centuries ago. The first games took place in Olympia in Western Greece. In the beginning, the games consisted only of one event, a foot-race of about 180 metres. But as time went on many other sports were added, such as chariot racing, javelin throwing, discus and wrestling.

Only the best athletes took part and coming first was all that mattered. The Greeks believed this was the best way to honour the god Zeus. The winner of each event received a simple olive wreath. Those who won were believed to be favoured by Zeus for the rest of their lives. The ancient Olympic Games were held every four years but in AD 394 they were stopped by the Roman emperor.

The Olympic Games Revived

In 1896 a Frenchman, Baron Pierre de Coubertin, revived the Olympic Games. The first modern games were held in Athens, Greece, and although only 13 countries took part, they were a huge success.

The Olympic Games Today

The Olympic Games are still held every four years but now they are in a different country each time. The country where they are held is called the host country. The host country may introduce a new sport. When the games were held in Tokyo, Japan, judo was introduced.

Only the best athletes from all over the world compete. Now, instead of an olive wreath the winner receives a gold medal. Those coming second and third receive silver and bronze respectively. Most of the old Olympic sports are still included but some new ones, such as soccer, tennis, gymnastics and basketball, have been added. In the winter of 1924, the first Winter Games were held. The Winter Games are usually held in a different country. Skiing, ice hockey and skating are some of the Winter Olympic events.

Do A. or B.

 A **Answer these questions.**

1. Where in Greece did the first Olympic Games take place?
2. Which Greek god did the Olympic Games honour?
3. What did the winners in the Olympic Games receive?
4. Name the Frenchman who revived the games.
5. In what year were the first Winter Olympics held?
6. What do we call the country where the games are held?

 B **Make three headings like those on page 28.**

Write down the main points from each paragraph under each heading. Use key words or phrases. The first has been started for you.

The First Olympic Games	The Olympic Games Revived	The Olympic Games Today
28 centuries ago Olympia, Western Greece		

 C **Use the information you have collected and write about one part of the Olympic Games to present to a group of children or your class.**

 D **Write about the other parts of the Olympic Games to present.**

Now find out more information about the Games. Use IT and the library.

Decide on one more heading. Note down the main points, write about them and add it to your work.

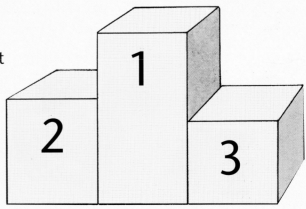

Speech Marks (1)

- Speech marks or inverted commas, as they are also called, are used to enclose the actual words spoken by a person or character.
- The first word inside speech marks should have a capital letter, e.g. "My homework is in my other bag," said Jenny.
- If speech is broken in two, the second part of speech need not have a capital letter, e.g. "My homework," said Jenny, "is in my other bag."
- All punctuation marks, such as question marks, exclamation marks, commas and full stops should be placed inside the speech marks, e.g. "When are you going to tell the truth?" asked the teacher.

 A **Write what each person said, using speech marks.**

Example: The judge asked, "How do you plead?"
"Not guilty," replied the accused.

 B **Write out the following sentences using speech marks.**

1. The thief admitted I stole the jewels.
2. Where are they now the detective inquired.
3. So this is your new house exclaimed my mother.
4. Dad won't let me do it moaned Peter.
5. Ann announced we're getting married in July.
6. I'm in right trouble now John lamented.
7. The General commanded let's move out now.
8. Are you going begged Deirdre please do.
9. The suspect protested don't tell me you think I did it.
10. The fire engulfed the building reported the journalist everything was destroyed.

Nouns

- A noun is the name of a person, place or thing.

Hello, my name is Mark.
I am from Kenya. I am an athlete.
I will be running in the Olympic Games.

 A **Write out the following sentences. Underline the nouns.**

1. There are many events in the Olympic Games.
2. Athletes from all over the world take part.
3. A man with a flaming torch runs on to the track.
4. He dips the torch into the bowl and the Olympic flame is lit.
5. The Olympic flag is white, with five rings in the centre.
6. Tessa put on her spikes and picked up her javelin.
7. The contestants skied down the mountain.
8. The athletes proudly accepted their medals.
9. The runners surged forward, eager to start the marathon.
10. The spectators stood as the winner entered the stadium.

 B **Using the nouns you've underlined, write eight sentences about the Olympic Games.**

The Olympic Games ...

 C **How many nouns can you list under the following headings?**

Capital cities	Olympic events	Countries
Madrid	marathon	Canada

Keep a Poem in Your Pocket

Keep a poem in your pocket
and a picture in your head
and you'll never feel lonely
at night when you're in bed.

The little poem will sing to you
the little picture bring to you
a dozen dreams to dance to you
at night when you're in bed.

So—
Keep a picture in your pocket
and a poem in your head
and you'll never feel lonely
at night when you're in bed.

Beatrice Schenk de Regniers

 Answer these questions.

1. What poem would you keep in your pocket? Why?
2. What picture would you keep? Why?
3. What is the first poem you remember from when you were little? What do you like about it?

 Read the poem aloud.

Write down the words that rhyme with each other. Remember to check the middle of the lines as well as the end.

C Say these groups of words.

| poem   pocket   picture | | dozen   dreams |

What letters do they have in common?

In Formation

1. What is happening in this picture? Describe the aeroplanes in detail.

2. How many 'Red Arrows' can you see? Do you think there are more in the team?

3. Why are they flying like this do you think? Are they perhaps training, giving a display or flying a mission?

4. What is the smoke coming out of the back of the aeroplanes for?

5. Do you think flying like this is difficult? Is it dangerous? Would the pilots need a lot of training? Why? Do you think the pilots are brave?

6. Have you ever been to an air display? What was it like? How many aeroplanes did you see? What sounds did the crowd make?

7. Have you ever been in an aeroplane? Do you think it was like flying in a 'Red Arrow'? What could you see from the air? Would you like to fly an aeroplane? Why?

The Adventures of Young Fionn

When Fionn was a baby his father Cumhal was killed in battle. Muirne, Fionn's mother, took her son to the Slieve Bloom mountains, where he was looked after by two wise women. There in the fields, Fionn ran and played with the wild animals. Before long, he could outrun the fastest hare or deer. In the streams and rivers he swam as swiftly as the fish. Fionn loved games. His favourite was hurling. He grew up brave and strong.

At last the wise women decided it was time for Fionn to find his Uncle Crimhall, who, they believed, lived in Connaught. So, sadly, Fionn left the Slieve Bloom mountains and set out for Connaught. On his way, he met some boys swimming in a lake and he was able to swim faster than any of them. Next, he met a woman who wept for her dead son. He had been killed by a champion who lived nearby. Fionn fought and killed the champion. This man had a magical bag which Fionn took. The bag helped Fionn find his Uncle Crimhall.

By now Fionn was hungry for more knowledge. He went to a poet called Finegas who lived near the River Boyne. Finegas had spent all his life fishing for the Salmon of Knowledge. He told Fionn that the first person who tasted the salmon would become the wisest person in the land.

One fine day, Finegas did indeed catch the fish. He gave it to Fionn to cook and warned him not to eat any. While the fish was cooking a blister rose on it. Fionn touched it and burned his right thumb. He then sucked his thumb to ease the pain. Finegas was very upset when he heard this because Fionn was now the wisest man in the land.

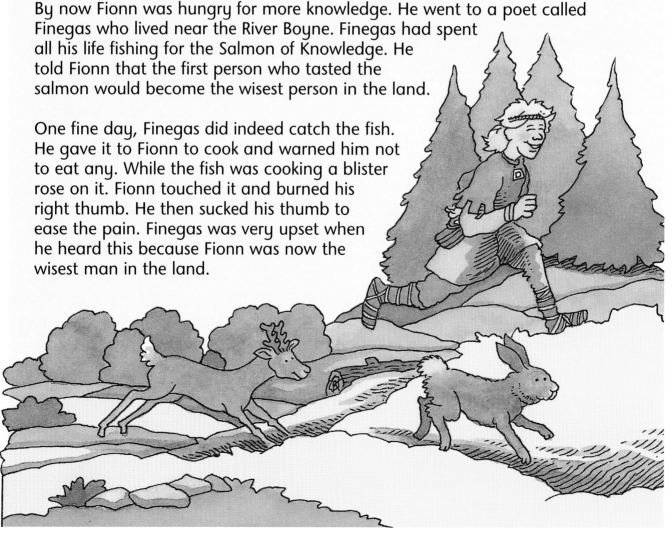

A Answer these questions.

1. Name Fionn's father and mother.
2. Where did Fionn's mother take him after his father's death?
3. What was Fionn's favourite sport?
4. Why do you think the wise women thought it was time for Fionn to find his uncle?
5. How do you think the magical bag helped Fionn?
6. Why did Fionn go to Finegas?

B Read the last paragraph of the story again. Compare it to the playscript below. List all the ways in which the playscript is different.

Fionn is a clever and brave young man. Finegas is a poet who has spent all his life fishing for the Salmon of Knowledge. One day he catches the fish. He turns to Fionn.

Finegas: Remember, Fionn, when you cook this salmon you must not eat any, not even a tiny bit.

Fionn: _____

● Now finish the playscript, using your own words for the dialogue.

C Rewrite the story.

The Adventures of Young Fionn is a traditional Irish folk tale. Rewrite the story so it takes place in the area where you live. Think about people's names, places, rivers, mountains. Begin by describing the **setting** of your story carefully.

Shape Poems

 Look at these acrostics, then try some of your own.

Patient
   Approachable
     Responsible
    Efficient
    Nervous
     Terrified
    Suspicious

Delicious
  Incredible
   Necessary
   Nutty
    Enough
     Recover

 A lantern poem has five lines arranged in the order below. Look at the example and try one of your own.

1st line – one syllable   Sport
2nd line – two syllables   Running
3rd line – three syllables   High-Jumping
4th line – four syllables   Relay-Racing
5th line – one syllable   Rest

In a concrete poem the layout of the words reflect the subject. This example is written inside a picture, but this is not always the case.

Now you try one.

 Parodies.

- Parodies are great fun. Simply substitute different words for some in a well-known poem. Look at this example, then try one of your own.

    'Twas an hour before my wedding,
    And all through the house,
    My mother was screaming,
    "Where's my polka-dot blouse?"

Verbs

- A verb is an action word.
  The teacher **read** the book. Bards **travelled** from house to house.
- Before the days of television, people loved hearing the tales of a storyteller.

Copy the following passage and circle the verbs.

A They placed the stools and chairs around the warm fire. The kettle boiled cheerily on the hob. The men smoked their pipes while the women busied themselves making tea and pouring whiskey. Soon they all sat down. The storyteller had arrived. Simon threw a log on the fire and settled back to listen to the story. Claire closed her eyes. She lay on the straw bed. She could hear the drone of the storyteller's voice and wished she was old enough to stay up for the story. The lilting tones of the voice below soon lulled her to sleep.

B **Here is the beginning of the storyteller's story. Choose suitable verbs to fill the gaps.**

One fine summer's day, two children were _____ by a stream. Suddenly they _____ a strange little man _____ in the water. He _____ so odd that they began to _____ at him. The goblin (for that's what he was) _____ very angry and used his magic on them. The children _____ smaller and smaller until they _____ the same size as the goblin.

C **Write out the sentences, inserting a suitable verb.**

1. The tired old horse (galloped/stumbled) along the path.
2. The ferocious lion (squealed/roared) in pain.
3. The hungry bear (nibbled/devoured) the meat.

D **Put the following verbs into sentences.**

huddled   sheltered   received   rescue   hoard

The Past Tense

- Remember, when something has happened, it is written in the past tense.
- Most stories are written in the past tense.

 Write out the following story, choosing the correct word in the past tense.

What a time I *(have/had)* on Saturday. I *(went/go)* to see my favourite team play. It *(is/was)* very exciting. Half way through the game the ball *(fly/flew)* into the crowd. I *(saw/see)* it in the air, *(catch/caught)* it and *(throw/threw)* it back straight away.
   Everybody *(cheered/cheers)*! Although my team *(did/does)* not win, I *(was/is)* not too unhappy, for once.

 Add another paragraph in the past tense about what you told your teacher when you returned to school on Monday.

 When we add ing to a verb it can alter the spelling like this:

hop + ing = hopping   We double the letter.

Add **ing** to these words and write them out correctly.
pat   clap   let   pin   win   skip   swim   rot   run
Write them in sentences. You can write more than one word in a sentence.

D **Not all verbs change. We write:**

seeing   feeling   cooking

If it helps, remember this rule:
When a word has a short vowel sound before one last consonant we double the consonant when adding **ing**.

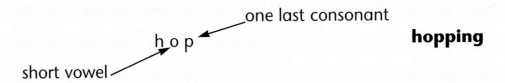

Save the Elephant

 A **Read the poster below.**

- The main message is in big black letters so people can see it easily. If you can think up something short and catchy to attract people's attention, they will stop and read the rest of the poster.

- Bring in a selection of posters and advertisements to school. Discuss each one. Look at how they are designed.

B **Design:**

- A save the elephant poster.
  These words might help: protect, needless, slaughter, endangered species, don't buy ivory, leave the ornaments behind.

C **Write:**

- A letter to your M.P. asking for action to stop the ivory trade and punish anyone who trades in it.

Tiny Tim's Christmas

In came Bob; his threadbare clothes darned up and brushed to look seasonable; and Tiny Tim upon his shoulder. Alas for Tiny Tim, he bore a little crutch, and had his limbs supported by an iron frame.

"And how did little Tim behave?" asked Mrs Cratchit as the two young Cratchits bore Tiny Tim off to hear the pudding sing in the copper.

"As good as gold," said Bob. "He told me, coming home, that he hoped the people saw him in church, because it might be pleasant for them to remember upon Christmas Day who made lame beggars walk and blind men see."

Bob's voice was shaking when he told them this, and shook more when he said that Tiny Tim was growing strong and hearty.

Back came Tiny Tim before another word was spoken, and Master Peter and the two young Cratchits went to fetch the goose, with which they soon returned.

There was such a bustle that you might have thought a goose the rarest of birds; and in truth it was something very like it in that house. At last the dishes were set on, and grace was said. It was succeeded by a breathless pause, as Mrs Cratchit, looking slowly all along the carving knife, prepared to plunge it in the breast; but when she did, and the long-expected gush of stuffing issued forth, one murmur of delight arose all around, and even Tiny Tim feebly cried "Hurrah!"

There was never such a goose. Bob said he didn't believe there ever was such a goose cooked. Together with the apple sauce and mashed potatoes, it was a sufficient dinner for the whole family; indeed, as Mrs Cratchit said (surveying one small atom of a bone upon the dish), they hadn't ate it all yet!

Charles Dickens

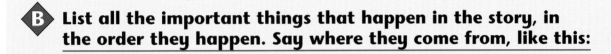

A **Answer these questions.**

1. What was Mr Cratchit's first name?
2. How did Tiny Tim behave when he was out with his father?
3. Why do you think Bob's voice was shaking when he spoke about Tiny Tim?
4. What food did the Cratchits have for Christmas?
5. Describe the goose.
6. If Tiny Tim was granted one wish for Christmas, what might it be?
7. Tiny Tim is in a story written by Charles Dickens. Find out the name of the story.
8. Find these words in the passage and decide what they mean:
   threadbare, seasonable, bustle, rarest, succeeded, breathless, plunge, atom.
   Check them in a dictionary.

B **List all the important things that happen in the story, in the order they happen. Say where they come from, like this:**

1. Bob comes home with Tiny Tim.   Paragraph 1.
2. .....

C **Make a character portrait of Tiny Tim.**

Draw your own picture of Tiny Tim.
List what he looks like on one side of your picture. List what sort of person he is on the other side.

What he looks like      **What he is like**

D **Now do the same for Bob.**

Contractions (1)

 When we talk we often make two words into one word.

It's raining!

What we really mean is: **It is** raining!

When we write, we use an apostrophe to show what letters are missing.

It is   It is   =   It's

● Words like this are called contractions.

 Match these words to their contractions by writing them out together. Underline the letters that are lost. What do we put in their place?

I am	isn't
let us	don't
is not	he's
do not	wasn't
he is	let's
was not	I'm

 Work out the two words from these contractions and write them out.

1. I've   **2.** We'll   **3.** We've

4. can't   **5.** What's   **6.** You're

7. she'll   **8.** They're   **9.** They've

 Choose five contractions and write five sentences with them in.

Grammar

Capital Letters (3)

You will remember that a capital letter is always used:
- At the start of a sentence.
- For names of people, personal titles and places.
- For the name of a day and a month.
- For headings and book titles.
- Don't forget that 'I' on its own is always written with a capital letter, too.

 Write out the following letter correctly. Some of the capital letters have been left out.

2 cobble Lane
Horse street
ridington
thursday april 4th

Dear Auntie cissy

i have something important to tell you...

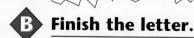 **Finish the letter.**

C **Capital letters are also used at the beginning of each line of a poem and also when we want to stress something (give it special emphasis).**

Read the beginning of this poem, write it out and finish it. Add more verses if you want. Note that the beginning of each word in the title of the poem also has a capital letter.

In The Middle
My little sister always
SHOUTS SHOUTS SHOUTS,
My older brother's always
OUT OUT OUT,
My Mum is always moaning,
And my Dad is always groaning,
BUT my Gran is _____ .

43

Writing a Menu

 A The Cratchit children designed this menu for their Christmas dinner. Make a menu for Sam Snowman's Christmas dinner. You could include icicle pops, snowflakes, milk and iced tea.

 B Now design a menu for:

1. The Cratchit dog's Christmas dinner.
2. Rudolph's Christmas dinner.

● Remember to use capital letter for words that have special emphasis.

MAIN COURSE
Hot Roast Goose
stuffed with Sage and Onion
Apple Sauce
Mashed Potatoes
❄ ❄ ❄

DESSERT
Christmas Pudding
in Brandy Sauce
❄ ❄ ❄

A Busy Street

1. Describe the picture. What time of year is it? How do you know? Do you like this time of year? Why? The street is very busy. Where do you think the people in the buses are going? What type of precautions should you take when shopping in a busy street?

2. What preparations do people make for Christmas? What preparations do shopkeepers make? When do you think they start getting ready? Where do you do your Christmas shopping? What presents would you like to buy your family? What presents do you hope to get? Will every child in the world receive Christmas presents? Will everybody sit down to a nice meal? Explain your answers.

3. Make a list of some ways you can help people less fortunate than you at Christmas.

The Robin

In spring the hen and cock robin build their nest in a bush or shrub. The hen does most of the work while the cock looks on, singing happily. Their nest is in the shape of a bowl and is made with moss, grass, twigs and leaves. The inside is lined with mud and over this the birds place pieces of grass. The mother robin lays between three and seven white eggs. She then sits on them to keep them warm. After about two weeks, the eggs hatch. The baby robins peck out of the shells. Anyone in difficulty is helped along by the mother.

At first the nestlings have no feathers. Their eyes are closed and they are very weak and helpless. They are always hungry. The mother and father robin find themselves very busy collecting worms and wriggly caterpillars to feed their young. The robin's bill is shaped like tweezers and this makes it easier to pick up the food from the ground.

Every day the nestlings grow bigger and stronger. Before long they are covered with speckled brown feathers. Then they start learning how to fly. The mother and father robin continue to feed the nestlings until they are able to fly and find their own food. When this happens, it is time for the young robins to leave the nest.

Robins stay with us all year round but because they can be seen searching for food in our gardens and on our bird tables all through the winter they have become associated with Christmas. The snow and ice make it difficult for the birds to find food and water. So don't forget to feed the birds during the winter months.

A Answer these questions.

1. When does the robin build her nest?
2. How long does it take for the robin's eggs to hatch?
3. What is the robin's bill shaped like?
4. What food does a robin eat?
5. How can we help birds in the winter?
6. Make a list of food you would leave on the bird table.

B Read the first paragraph again, to check what the robin's nest is made of.

Draw a robin's nest.
Label your drawing using arrows.

C Write down and complete this writing frame about the nestlings. Use your own words.

At first the nestlings _____

The mother and father robin _____

Every day the nestlings _____

When the nestlings learn _____

D Find out about migration. Use these keywords and phrases to help you. Write a paragraph in your own words.

winter   colder   warmer   countries   return

47

Silent Letters – w, k, l and h

A **Put the w in each word. Read them aloud.**

These words all have a silent **w**.

s _ ord

_ rite

_ reck

B **k is silent in all these words. Read each one aloud.**

knot	knit	know	knew	knife	kneel
knee	knave	knock	knuckle	knob	knowledge

C **Write out these sentences. Complete them using the words in the box. Which letter is silent in each word?**

1. A _____ is a baby cow.
2. I will eat _____ the sweets now.
3. Mum will _____ to you after school.
4. We went for a _____ in the country.
5. The _____ of an egg is yellow.
6. The sea was _____ after the storm.
7. You _____ eat your vegetables.
8. I _____ love to go to your party.

calm
calf
yolk
should
would
half
walk
talk

D **h is silent in all these words. Write each sentence, using words from the box to fill the spaces. Read each sentence aloud.**

1. It is dis_____ to tell a lie.
2. The _____ haunted the castle.
3. The party will begin in one _____ .
4. I don't go to _____ on Sunday.
5. We didn't see the _____ when we visited the zoo.
6. He sailed from the boat in a _____ .

hour
ghost
rhinoceros
dinghy
school
honest

Silent Letters – b, g, u and t

A **In all these words b is silent. Read each one aloud.**

debt   lamb   thumb   numb   plumber   doubt   climb   comb

B **Write out the words, filling in the missing b. Make two lists: words with a silent b and those without.**

lam _   _ one   tu _   plum _ er   com _

ro _ ot   lim _   crum _   ri _ _ on   clim _

C **In all these words u is silent. Read each one aloud. Make up sentences with some of the words.**

guitar   biscuit   buoy   guy   guest   guess

D **Select suitable words from the box to complete the sentences below. Read each sentence aloud.**

1. I was bitten by a _____.
2. Mum put the _____ in the garden.
3. The king will _____ for a long time.
4. The angry lion was _____ his teeth.

reign
gnashing
gnat
gnome

E **Choose the correct words from the box to complete the sentences.**

1. The queen lives in a _____.
2. _____ and you will hear.
3. The referee blew the _____.
4. My dad has _____ on his chin.
5. The _____ is the national emblem of Scotland.

whistle
bristles
castle
thistle
listen

49

Singular and Plural of Nouns (1)

- Singular means one.
- Plural means more than one.

| mountain | mountains |
| stream | streams |

 Copy these words and add s to make them plural.

son	lake
field	finger
animal	poet
river	battle
game	champion
boy	hare

 + es

- If a word ends in y after a consonant, change y to **i** and add **es**.
  Usually, if a word ends in f or fe, change f to **v** and add **es**.
  If a word ends in s, sh, ch or x, add **es**.

 Copy these words and make them plural.

baby	patch	stitch
knife	wife	box
thrush	penny	wolf

 Rewrite these sentences in the plural.

1. Fionn enjoyed the game of hurling.
2. He ran with the fox and the hare in the field.
3. He defeated the champion with the sword.
4. The boy scored the penalty.
5. The tall stork walked through the short grass.

Compound Words

- Sometimes we can put two small words together to make a bigger word.
- The complete word is called a **compound word**.

 A Break the compound words into two words, as in the example below.

1. blackbird   **black bird**
2. flagpole
3. birthday
4. inside
5. outside
6. hailstones
7. afternoon
8. maybe

9. bedroom
10. moonlight
11. handbag
12. sunflower
13. pancake
14. blackberry
15. toothbrush
16. seaside

 B Match the first and the second words. Write the new compound word.

A	B
sun	time
grass	day
bed	ball
basket	hopper

A	B
snow	fly
butter	noon
goal	ball
after	keeper

C In the following words, the second words are mixed up. Rewrite each word correctly.

up/time	bed/**set**	hail/side	birth/fighter
over/mate	in/stones	class/heard	fire/day

For example: upset

The Child Prodigy

Wolfgang Amadeus Mozart was born in Salzburg, Austria, in 1756. He learned to play the harpsichord (an instrument very like the piano) at the tender age of three. He was composing simple pieces of music when he was five and by the time he was six his father Leopold was taking him all over Europe, visiting many cities, including London, showing him off to kings and queens.

When he grew up Mozart was employed by the Archbishop of Salzburg. He stayed working for him until they quarrelled. Taking his wife Constanze with him, he went to Vienna to make his fortune. There he worked hard and many of his compositions were very successful. When Mozart was 31 his father, who owed a lot of money, died. Mozart was constantly working, travelling from city to city performing concerts and conducting. He was trying to earn enough money to pay off all his father's debts. He was composing all the time but remained very poor. A friend of Mozart's told this story:

"One winter's day, I called to visit my friend Wolfgang Amadeus Mozart. It was a very cold day and I found him at home, dancing with Constanze to keep warm, because they could not afford fuel for a fire!"

Mozart died in 1791 at the very young age of 35. He had composed over 150 orchestral works, as well as sonatas, string quartets and operas. The most famous of his operas are *The Marriage of Figaro*, *Don Giovanni* and *The Magic Flute*. Many people say he was the finest classical composer who ever lived.

A **Answer these questions.**

1. Where was Mozart born?
2. What is a harpsichord?
3. At what age did he learn to play the harpsichord?
4. Who was Mozart's first employer?
5. What was Mozart's wife called?
6. Why was Mozart poor?
7. What is an opera? Name three of Mozart's operas.
8. What do you think a 'child prodigy' is?

 B **Read the passage and complete this time line of Mozart's life. Write down what happened by each date.**

Mozart's Life
1756 –
1787 –
1791 –

C **Find the passage in which Mozart's friend tells a story. It is written as if he was speaking, that is, in the first person.**

Pretend you have seen Mozart play when he was six. You are telling a friend about it. Begin:

"Last night I went to see Mozart play! I could not believe he was only six because ... "

Finish the paragraph and read it out to a partner.

D **Do the same, pretending you are at Mozart's funeral. Remember he was only 35 when he died.**

Alphabetical Order (1)

 A **Say the alphabet aloud.**

1. Say it forwards.
2. Say it backwards.
3. Start at L.
4. Start at Q.

 B **Answer these questions.**

1. What letter comes after E?
2. What letter comes before O?
3. What letter comes two letters after R?
4. What letter comes two letters before W?
5. Before using a dictionary, you must know your alphabet. In a dictionary, words are arranged in alphabetical order. Where else are words organised alphabetically?

- These words are in alphabetical order. Look at the first letters.
  ask   boy   eager   giant   joyful

C **Write the following lists of words in alphabetical order.**

1. children, beautiful, garden.
2. song, flowers, birds.
3. snow, wind, rain.
4. wet, cold, miserable.
5. play, forever, years, nails, return.
6. dead, blossoms, paradise, winter, sad.
7. oak, sycamore, ash, beech, elm.
8. primrose, daisy, bluebell, foxglove, tulip.
9. robin, thrush, cuckoo, swallow, blackbird.
10. happy, sad, angry, worried, fearful.
11. giant, joy, beans, widow, cow.
12. skip, jump, hopscotch, races, play.

Alphabetical Order (2)

● When words have the same first letter, you look at the second letter to help you put them in alphabetical order.

 A **Rewrite the following lists of words in alphabetical order.**

1. brat, bend, blow.
2. fish, fry, fox.
3. trick, told, tan.
4. climb, chant, calm, circle, comfort.
5. island, ivory, inert, import, idea.
6. reduce, radio, rhyme, rock, ring.
7. squelch, shower, stake, screen, saw.
8. why, watch, wind, wrap, wear.

 B **When the first two letters are the same, look at the third letter.**

meal   medal   meet   member   menu   mess   metre

 C **Help your teacher organise the books in the library.**

Arrange the authors' surnames alphabetically.

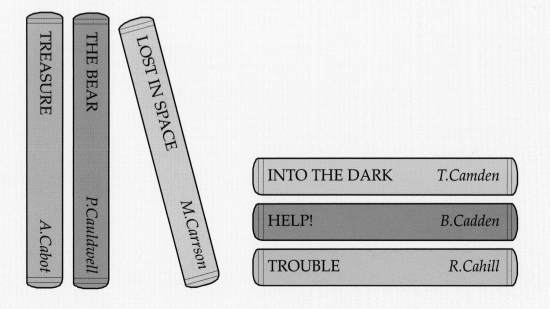

TREASURE — A.Cabot
THE BEAR — P.Cauldwell
LOST IN SPACE — M.Carryson
INTO THE DARK — T.Camden
HELP! — B.Cadden
TROUBLE — R.Cahill

Dictionary Work

 A **Put these words in order, as you would find them in the dictionary.**

1. hairy, mammal, higher, migrate, prodigy.
2. meander, excitement, merry, species, pleasure.
3. hibernate, yodel, homeless, yule, homily.
4. school, sofa, chair, chalk, toy.
5. animal, bear, alligator, chimpanzee, camel.
6. giraffe, German, ice, peppermint, geese.

 B **Copy the lists. Match the words on the left with the meanings on the right. Use your dictionary to help you. Write a sentence for each word.**

Word	Meaning
defer	fast
swift	to lose hair or feathers
howl	to put off or postpone
moult	to get worse
cautious	to gleam faintly
deteriorate	a deep, narrow gorge
bold	careful
ravine	brave
siesta	a long, doleful cry
token	a sign or symbol
glimmer	an afternoon nap or rest in hot countries

C **Open your dictionary at the letter g. List ten nouns.**

game ...

 D **Now write ten adjectives for these nouns.**

nouns	adjective
game	exciting

56

Suffixes

- A letter or a group of letters added on to the end of a root word is called a suffix. Look at what these suffixes do.

Suffix	Meaning	Example
1. -ful	full of/having	helpful
2. -y	full of/like	rusty
3. -less	without	careless
4. -ness	the state of being	ripeness
5. -ment	the result, act of	punishment

A **Rewrite the sentences. Choose the word with the correct suffix each time so that they make sense.**

1. The two chemicals produced a clear _____ liquid. (colourless, colouring)
2. The _____ of the sun dazzled my eyes. (brightless, brightness)
3. The judge announced her _____ after three hours. (judgeless, judgement)
4. As _____ fell, the moon and the stars appeared in the sky. (darkless, darkness)
5. It was a very _____ day, so I wore a jacket. (breezy, breezeless)
6. After four hours of talks, the two parties reached _____ . (agreement, agreeness).
7. My birthday party last week was _____ . (wondering, wonderful)

B **Rewrite the sentences. Use the clue after each sentence to decide which word is needed.**

1. The fox just lifted his _____ tail and walked quietly away. (like a bush)
2. Some air sprays are _____ to the Earth's ozone layer. (full of harm)
3. It was disappointing when the expert said that the painting was _____ . (without worth)
4. If my brother eats _____ foods, he immediately puts on weight. (full of fat)
5. The rainbow was extremely _____ . (having colour)
6. I thought the operation was _____ . (without pain)
7. My _____ of the film was ruined. (act of joy)

The Countryside in Spring

As we left the grey city and rode into the bright countryside, I listened for the sounds of spring. The birds were chirping, the bees were buzzing and the lambs bleating in the fields. We could see the farmers ploughing and sowing their crops, leaving deep furrows as they went.

We cycled on and I was amazed at the colour of the countryside. The yellow of the wild daffodils merged with the scarlet poppies and the golden catkins lined the hedgerows. In the distance I heard the sound of water and as we came closer I could see the crystal stream meandering through the field. The marsh-marigolds, their leaves shining, were swaying in the breeze.

We began to climb the steep hill and were startled to see hares bounding one after the other across the grass. Continuing our journey, we came to a wood. The trees towered above us and the light turned to dark. We could hear small creatures scurrying along and the undergrowth crackle. We hurried on until we emerged into the bright sunshine again. Looking down we could see the city beneath us, unfolding across the landscape.

Our descent was easier. We sailed down the hillside with the wind in our hair, hardly catching our breath. When we reached the bottom, we stopped at a shop and bought some ice cream, swirls of strawberry and vanilla that tasted good. We were tired but happy and felt that the cold, dreary winter days were over and that spring and new beginnings had arrived.

A **Answer these questions**

1. What type of transport was used in the story?
2. Make a list of the noises in the countryside.
3. What work does the farmer do in spring?
4. What was swaying in the breeze?
5. Why do you think the people hurried through the wood?
6. Why was the descent easier?
7. What was bought in the shop?
8. '… spring and new beginnings …'. What do you think this means?
9. Write down five adjectives from 'The Countryside in Spring'.

 B **Decide what you would need from the list below if you were going on a trip to the countryside. You will be catching a bus and walking.**

a recipe   a map   a plan   a poster   a timetable   a newspaper

Write down why you would need the things you have chosen.

 C **Some people prefer to live in the countryside. Others prefer to live in the city.**

Draw a chart like the one below with two columns. List three points in favour of the city under 'For' and three in the 'Against' column. Don't forget to number your points.

Living in the City

For   Against

1 _____   1 _____

2 _____   2 _____

3 _____   3 _____

 D **Write a paragraph saying whether you would prefer to live in the countryside or the city.**

Explain why.

Adjectives

- Adjectives are describing words. They tell us more about the noun,
  e.g. a **babbling** brook   the **shy little** boy
- We use paints to colour a picture.
- We use adjectives to colour a sentence.

 Copy these phrases and underline those that are 'coloured in'.

1. the dancing red poppies
2. the man
3. a cunning sly fox
4. a shy embarrassed boy
5. the accident
6. a tiger
7. the night
8. a lively playful puppy
9. the alien
10. a dark frightening cave

Add 'colour' to the phrases you didn't underline.

 Write out the passage. Underline the adjectives.

Spring is a very busy time. The dark dreary winter has gone and the colourful flowers arrive to cheer us up. The shy white snowdrop and the pretty crocus are the first to appear. The little birds build their nests and sing happily as they work. The handsome red squirrel and the prickly hedgehog wake from their long winter's sleep. Delicate buds appear on the trees. Spring is a happy season when nature comes to life again.

 You will find adjectives in the petals and nouns in the centre of the flowers. How many sentences can you make?

The **tiny** boy walked through the **gloomy** forest.

Word Endings

Some words change when we add er or est: big
We double the letter: big + est = biggest   big + er   =   bigger

 A Draw this diagram and make new words in the same way:

	er	est
big	bigger	biggest
hot		
mad		
red		
fit		
flat		
thin		

Choose four words and write sentences for each word.

B The same happens with some words if we add y.

chat + y = chatty   We double the letter.
Write the answers to these word sums in your book.
flop + y =   Mum + y =
Dad + y =   Gran + y =

 C Write out these, putting in the missing letters.

A pe _ _ y or a pound?   The flo _ _ y bu _ _ y
Mole and Ra _ _ y   My Gra _ _ y

D Not all words that end in y double the letter: baby lady tiny.

Remember the rule:
When a word has a **short** vowel sound before one last consonant we
usually double the consonant before adding er, est or y.
Exception: copy

Singular and Plural of Nouns (2)

● Some words ending in **o** get their plural by adding **-es** and some get their plural by just adding **-s**.

 A **Write the plurals of the following words.**

+s		+es	
banjo	dynamo	hero	tornado
video	cello	volcano	domino
photo	torso	echo	cargo
cuckoo		tomato	

 B **Here are some words that change completely! Write out their plurals. Can you fill in the gaps?**

Singular	Plural	Singular	Plural
man	men	tooth	teeth
woman		foot	
mouse	mice	goose	

 C **These words stay the same! Write a sentence for each word.**

sheep	salmon	fish	cod	trout	deer	scissors

 D **Rewrite these sentences in the singular.**

1. The red deer ran into the fields.
2. I watched the robins on the branches.
3. The boys were heroes.
4. Fionn burned his fingers and tasted the salmon.
5. The mice ran over the women's feet.
6. The men fell and broke their teeth.
7. I saw the photos on the shelves.
8. I will eat the potatoes and the tomatoes.

Bird Feeder

1. Describe what is happening in the picture. What type of bird is this? What time of the year is it? What food is the bird eating? What other kind of food could you leave out for the birds? Why do we feed the birds in this season?

2. Who do you think left out the food? Has this bird got a family? Is the bird hungry? When might it have eaten last? Why is the food placed so high up off the ground? Why do you think there are no other birds in the picture? Have they been frightened away? What might have frightened them?

3. Fill a net with bird food and hang it from a branch. Observe how many birds visit your garden in one week and make a list of them.

The History of Space Travel

There are nine known planets in our solar system. They are Mercury, Venus, Earth, Mars, Jupiter, Saturn, Uranus, Neptune and Pluto. For many years people have dreamed of leaving Earth and exploring space. During World War II (1939–1945) the Germans developed a new kind of rocket and this made space travel possible.

It wasn't until 1957 that the Space Age really began. The Russians launched the first artificial satellite, *Sputnik I*. Shortly after this, the first living creature, a dog called Laika, was sent by the Russians into space. On 12 April 1961, Yuri Gagarin became the first person in space. The Russians called him a cosmonaut (a space sailor). His craft made one complete orbit of the Earth. This took one hour and 29 minutes. About two weeks later, an American astronaut, Alan Bartlett Shepard Jr, became the second person to go into space. By the middle of 1963, a dozen people had travelled into space and returned safely. Among them was Valentina Tereshkova, a Russian cosmonaut who became the first woman in space.

Now a race between America and Russia was on. Who would send the first person to the Moon? On 16 July 1969, *Apollo II* was launched by the Americans. It reached the Moon on 20 July. Neil Armstrong was the first person to step out from the space module, nicknamed *The Eagle*. As he put his foot on the Moon he said, "*The Eagle* has landed. That's one small step for man – one giant leap for mankind." Buzz Aldrin followed him out and placed an American flag on the Moon. The race had been won!

Answer these questions.

1. What nation launched the first artificial satellite? What was it called?
2. What is a cosmonaut?
3. What does 'orbit' mean? Check in a dictionary.
4. How long did it take to orbit the Earth?

 Find a diagram of the solar system. You will need to look in the library or use IT.

Copy the diagram and label the planets, using arrows.

 Read the passage and complete the time line. Write down what happened next to each date.

The History of Space Travel
1939 – 1945
1957 –
1961 –
1963 –
1969 –

 Write down and complete this writing frame about the Space Race. Use your own words.

The Space Race was between …
They wanted to be the first to …
Apollo II …
Neil Armstrong …
Buzz Aldrin …
So, the first …

E **Imagine you are the first child in space.**

Write down what you will say to your family as you leave them to enter the space capsule.

The View from Space

1. Describe what you see. What is the satellite orbiting? What continent can you see?

2. This satellite sends and receives telephone, radio and television signals. Some satellites can also be used to monitor the weather or explore other planets. If you had a satellite, which planets would you use it to explore? What do you think you would see? Would you find life on another planet? What would it look like? Draw a picture.

3. Imagine you are an astronaut on your first mission in space. What preparations would you make? Describe what you are wearing. How do you feel before the blast off? What food do you eat? What things do you see? How do you feel when you get back? Is your family waiting?

4. Write a conversation between yourself and another astronaut who is flying with you.

Syllables (2)

● Some words can be divided into more than two syllables.

Meteorite has four syllables!

 Read aloud. How many syllables has each word got?

Jup-it-er   al-i-en   an-ten-na   gal-ax-y   as-tro-naut.

 Put the words into three lists: two syllables, three syllables and four syllables.

alien   planet   antenna
galaxy   terrestrial   meteorite
solar   astronaut   Venus
Tereshkova   shuttle   exploration
lunar   weightlessness atmospheric

two syllables	three syllables	four syllables
planet	alien	terrestrial

 Use your dictionary to help you find more words. List them under two syllables, three syllables and four syllables.

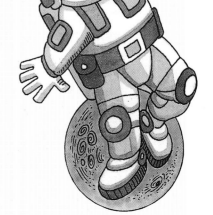

Sentence Building

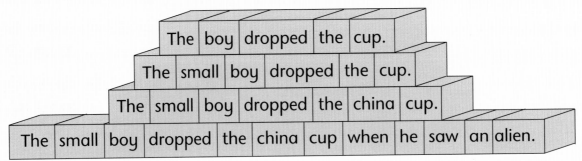

The boy dropped the cup.

The small boy dropped the cup.

The small boy dropped the china cup.

The small boy dropped the china cup when he saw an alien.

- You can build a sentence and make it more interesting if you ask yourself some questions about it, e.g. the boy dropped a cup.
Describe the boy: The small boy. Describe the cup: china cup.
Why did he drop it? Because he saw an alien.

A **Build up the following sentences. Write each one out.**

1. The astronaut stayed on the planet.

The _____ astronaut stayed on the _____ planet. (Describe (1) the astronaut, (2) the planet.)

The _____ astronaut stayed on the _____ planet for _____. (For how long?)

2. People have observed objects.

For _____ people have observed objects. (For how long have they observed objects?)

For _____ people have observed _____ objects. (Describe the objects.)

For _____ people have observed _____ objects _____. (Where?)

3. Jenny cried.

Jenny cried _____. (Describe how she cried.)

Jenny cried _____ because _____. (Why?)

B **Now build these sentences.**

1. The alien strolled.

2. The lion pounced.

3. The saucer landed.

4. The astronaut arrived home.

5. My goldfish died.

6. The fox killed.

Brainstorming

 A **Draw flying saucers and fill them with space words, as in the examples below.**

 B **Write six sentences describing the alien pictured. Build each sentence carefully.**

C **Finish this story.**

It was a bright, sunny day. Jennifer and Fatima were playing on the swings in the park. Suddenly, the sky darkened overhead. In the centre of the blackness a bright light appeared. The girls had to shield their eyes. As they looked, something fell from the sky. Jennifer and Fatima rushed to where it lay. A strange creature stood up, brushed himself down and said, 'Hi, I'm Al, an alien from outer space. Who are you?'

- Remember to check your work when finished.
- Give the story a title.

Letter from a Penpal

25 Rue de Rivoli
Paris
France
4-7-1998

Dear Emma

Thank you for your letter which I received yesterday. I really enjoyed reading it, as it was full of information about Britain. I hope that this letter will be as interesting for you and that I have answered all of the questions you asked about France.

The capital city is Paris, the city in which I live. Many people say that it is the most beautiful city in the world. It is built on the River Seine and is very famous for its roadside cafés and restaurants. Visitors who come here like to visit the Louvre, where they can see the original painting of the Mona Lisa. They also go to the Arc de Triomphe, the Eiffel Tower and Notre Dame Cathedral.

There are many mountains in France. In the winter French people like to go skiing in the snow-capped Alps. The Pyrenees mountains separate us from Spain. French people also like to drink wine and some of the finest vineyards in the world are here. The most famous French wine is Champagne and it comes from an area of the same name.

I was sad to hear that a lot of British people only speak English. Here in France, we all speak French and are very proud of it. It is our official language but there are several other languages and dialects such as Breton and Catalan to be heard in different parts of the country. We have a national day. It is on the 14th of July and is called Bastille Day. Our flag is a tricolour, blue, white and red.

I hope you have found this information interesting. Greetings to your parents and to your sisters, Sarah and Laura.

Write soon!

Au revoir
Françoise

First read the letter on page 70. Then answer these questions.

1. Where does Françoise live?
2. On what river is Paris built?
3. What is the Louvre?
4. Name some famous tourist sights.
5. Find Paris on a map of France.

Personal Pronouns

 Read this sentence.

The dog ran up the road and turned the corner as the dog reached home.
It would be better to say:
The dog ran up the road and turned the corner as it reached home.
We can use **it** instead of **the dog**. **It** is a pronoun.
We can use pronouns instead of nouns.

 Find these pronouns in the letter from Françoise. They are personal pronouns:

I   you   it   we   they: Write down who or what they stand for.
He, she, me, him, her, us and **them** are also personal pronouns.

Write out the following, putting the pronouns in the correct places. The first has been done for you.

Ray told <u>us</u> that _____ had lost his bag. It was the bag his sister had given _____ for his birthday. He explained that _____ had spent _____ time and money choosing the right one and asked _____ if I could help find _____ . He added that all his books were inside and he needed _____ for school.

Four of the pronouns in C are referring to male and female. We call this gender. Write down the pronouns, saying what gender they are.

Look at D. again. What person is it written in, the First person 'I' or the Third person 'he'?

71

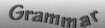

Possessive Pronouns

 Read this sentence.

My dog loves to chew his bone.
My shows that the dog belongs to me.
His shows that the bone belongs to the dog.
My and his are possessive pronouns.

   1. Find these possessive pronouns in the letter from Françoise on page 70:
      your   our
    Write down what they show.

mine, **yours**, **her**, **hers**, **ours**, **their**, **theirs**, **its** are also possessive pronouns.

 **Write out the following, putting the pronouns in
the correct places. Choose from the pronouns above.**

Will you swap your red pen for my blue one? I think _____ has a better
top, but I prefer _____ , because it is a brighter colour. Of course, Sally's
pen is the best of all because _____ is new. Sonia and Susan also have
good pens, but _____ are too small for me.

   1. What gender are the pronouns in the passage? How do you know?
   2. Look at the passage again. What person is it written in, the First person
      'I' or the Third person 'she'?

C **Pretend you are Emma. Write a reply to
Françoise telling her about school in Britain.**

Use personal pronouns such as she and he, as well as I and you. Use
possessive pronouns such as my and yours. Begin your letter like this:

Dear Françoise

Thank you for your last letter. Paris sounds very beautiful. I would
love to see it. Today, I am going to tell you about my school ...

Letter Writing

● Let us look at the way Françoise wrote her letter.

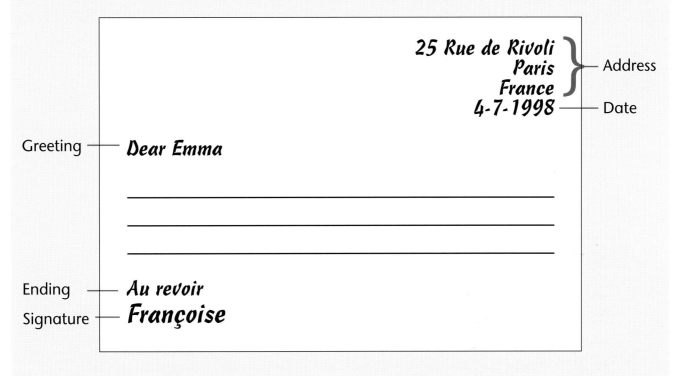

25 Rue de Rivoli
Paris } — Address
France }
4-7-1998 — Date

Greeting — *Dear Emma*

_____
_____
_____

Ending — *Au revoir*
Signature — *Françoise*

1. Always place your address in the top right-hand corner.
2. Under the address, write the date.
3. Write your greeting on the left-hand side of the letter.
4. Françoise ended her letter with 'Au revoir'. There are many other ways to do this: Yours sincerely, Yours faithfully, Best wishes, Your good friend, Your loving nephew/daughter etc.

 Imagine you are Emma. Write a short note to Françoise inviting her to your country on a holiday.

Remember to address the letter correctly.

 Now, write short letters from Françoise.

1. Accepting the invitation.
2. Declining the invitation.

Contractions

- When we speak we often link words together.
- When two words are joined together, the apostrophe is used for the missing letter or letters, e.g. They + will = They'll

 Write a contraction for these words below.

1. She is
2. Could not
3. I am
4. You have
5. What is
6. Do not
7. You will
8. Shall not
9. We are
10. Let us
11. It is
12. They are not
13. Should not
14. That is
15. Cannot

 Rewrite the following sentences using contractions.

1. There is a new cinema opening and it is awesome.
2. I would like to go to it, but I am broke.
3. If it is not raining, we will walk.
4. Thomas will not walk though, as he is lazy.
5. Who is knocking at the door?
6. What is the matter? Can you not find the key?
7. We will be late, if you do not hurry up.
8. I have no choice. I will have to go.

C Watch out! Some contractions have more than one meaning. Look at the examples.

He's could mean he has or he is.
I'd could mean I had, I should or I would.
What's could mean what is or what has.

D Decide what each of these contractions means.

1. I'd come to see you but I don't have the time.
2. What's Adam got in his pockets?
3. What's that dog doing?
4. If he's forgotten to take his sports kit he'll be in trouble.

74

Letter to a Penpal

- In the opening paragraph of her letter, Françoise thanks Emma for the letter she had received which was full of information about Britain.

 What do you think Emma told Françoise about Britain?

Gather as much information as you can.

1. What countries make up the British Isles?
2. What are the capital cities?
3. Describe the Union Flag, the flag of the United Kingdom.
4. What sights are to be seen in London?
5. What do you know about: (i) the Tower of London? (ii) Buckingham Palace?
6. What type of weather does Britain have?
7. Where do people go on holidays in Britain?
8. Describe the scenery around your area.
9. What is your home town famous for?

B **Having gathered all this information:**

1. Write Emma's letter to Françoise. Françoise says in her letter, 'I hope I have answered all of the questions you asked about France'. Remember to include these questions.
2. Design a poster advertising holidays in Britain.
   These phrases might help:
   - beautiful scenery
   - good fun
   - friendly people
   - great variety
   - unspoilt countryside.

Demand for a Cat Star

The schoolmistress cat began her lecture. "Look up there," she pointed with her paw. "That constellation is The Great Bear and over there is The Small Bear. Turn around when I do. Can you see, just at the right of the Argentine Tower, the Dragon Star? Then, there's Capricorn, Aries and Scorpio," continued the school-mistress cat. "And that one is the Dog Star."

"Well, I never!" expostulated the proper cats. "A Dog Star!" The one muttering and rumbling the loudest was a cat known as The Red Pirate.
"Well, where's the Cat Star?" he asked.
"There isn't one," replied the schoolmistress cat rather lamely.
"No Cat Star? Not even one tiny one called the Cat Star?" cried The Red Pirate.
"No, I'm afraid not."
"In other words," burst out The Red Pirate, "they've given stars to dogs and bears and any number of other animals, but no star to us cats. What a rotten deal."

Miaows of protest could be heard. The schoolmistress cat raised her voice to defend astronomers and their stars, saying that if astronomers believed you shouldn't name an asteroid after a cat, then they must have very good reasons. But the assembly disagreed and decided to organise a demonstration of protest. Special messages were sent by courier to all the cats in Rome. The time was set for midday at the Colosseum.

The next morning, many visitors and tourists turned up at the Colosseum on sight-seeing tours. There were Americans in cars, Germans in coaches, Swiss with leather handbags and of course Italians. But none of them could see the Colosseum because it was completely covered in cats.

Cats occupied the entrances, exits, arena, steps, columns and arches. You couldn't see any of the ancient stones. All that could be seen was thousands of cats. A large banner was brought out and unfurled. It read, 'Occupation of Colosseum. We demand a Cat Star.' Tourists, visitors and passers-by stopped and all applauded enthusiastically. It was a great occasion.

Before long, excitement developed on an international scale. The cats planned to occupy all the most famous places in the world: The Eiffel Tower, Big Ben, The Empire State Building ... They brought their request before astronomers of all nationalities and languages.

One day – No! One night – a Cat Star would shine with its own brilliance.

A Answer these questions.

1. On what subject was the schoolmistress cat talking?

2. List the stars and constellations she pointed out.

3. What were the cats complaining about?

4. Who spoke the loudest?

5. What did the cats decide to do?

6. Who turned up at the Colosseum the next morning?

7. Name the famous places the cats were going to visit.

8. Do you think the cats were serious about getting their own star? Explain why.

9. Do you think this story could take place in real life? Explain your answer.

10. Find out the meaning of:

constellation   astronomer   astrology   horoscope

asteroid   demonstration   protest

11. What was the Colosseum and where is it?

 B Messages were sent to all the cats in Rome about the demonstration. Write the message The Red Pirate might have sent to his friend.

Give the friend a name.

 C Pretend you were one of the cats in the classroom.

Tell the beginning of the story in your own words. Use the First person, 'I'. You could start like this. Write a paragraph.

I could not believe it! How could there be a Dog Star but no Cat Star? I decided ...

 D Continue with the story. Plan two more paragraphs.

Use a writing frame to help you.

Speech Marks (2)

- (a) "That constellation is The Great Bear and over there is The Small Bear,"said the schoolmistress cat.

  (b) The Red Pirate asked, "Well, where's the Cat Star?"
- Only the spoken words are written 'inside' the speech marks.

 Write out these sentences correctly. Insert speech marks, commas, full stops and question marks where needed.

1. One of these days I'll go off and join the cats said Signor Antonio
2. Do you know who I am she asked
3. This evening there's going to be a discussion on astronomy explained the cat
4. Did you know that the star clusters around Andromeda look just like commas said Signor Antonio
5. I sentence all astronomers to a plague the Judge Cat pronounced
6. Wouldn't it be marvellous he remarked to see the Dome of Saint Peter's in Rome decorated with cats
7. Look up there she said and pointed with her paw
8. They've given no stars to cats hissed the Red Pirate can you believe it

 Rewrite the following paragraph, inserting capital letters, full stops, commas and speech marks where needed.

he made his way to argentina square where among the ruins of ancient rome sat cats galore the first thing he did was to lick his paws to make quite sure that no dust from his human shoes followed him into his new life almost immediately a mangy lady cat came up to him she stared at him straight in the face until she finally said excuse me weren't you signor antonio i don't ever want to be a human being again he replied i've just handed in my notice to the human race ah just as i thought purred the lady cat i'm the schoolmistress who lived in the boarding house opposite your home ah yes said signor antonio you and your sister were always fighting about those canaries

Exaggeration

- A good storyteller exaggerates when telling a tale. This keeps the readers interested, even if they don't believe what they are reading.
- Usually there is some truth in the story.

 Read the passage below.

The fisherman had just returned from a fishing trip. He had been caught at sea in the middle of a storm. When he returned, he told his family, "The storm started suddenly. I wasn't expecting it. The boat was rocked back and forth by the gale force winds. A gigantic wave, bigger than the boat itself, lifted the vessel into the air. I managed, however, to keep her afloat. It was a narrow escape. When everything calmed down, I continued to fish and hooked an enormous swordfish, but as I reeled him in he escaped and fell back into the sea!"

 What do you think?

1. Was there a storm?
2. Did a gigantic wave, bigger than the boat itself, lift the vessel into the air?
3. If it did, could one man manage to keep the boat afloat?
4. Did the fisherman calmly resume fishing after having such a lucky escape?
5. Did he catch the enormous fish?
6. Write what you think really did happen.

Kidnapped!

This morning I got kidnapped
By three masked men.
They stopped me on the sidewalk,
And offered me some candy,
And when I wouldn't take it
They grabbed me by the collar,
And pinned my arms behind me,
And shoved me in the backseat
Of this big black limousine and
Tied my hands behind my back
With sharp and rusty wire.
Then they put a blindfold on me
So I couldn't see where they took me,
And plugged up my ears with cotton
So I couldn't hear their voices.
And drove for 20 miles or
At least for 20 minutes, and then
Dragged me from the car down to
Some cold and mouldy basement,
Where they stuck me in the corner
And went off to get the ransom
Leaving one of them to guard me
With a shotgun pointed at me,
Tied up sitting on a stool...
That's why I'm late for school!

Shel Silverstein